Stop Slicing in Five Swings

The Seven Golf Myths That Are Destroying Your Game

Scott Seifferlein

Copyright © 2012 by Scott Seifferlein

This is a work nonfiction. Any resemblance to actual persons, organizations, or events are purely coincidence.

All rights reserved by the author, including the right of reproduction in whole or in part in any form.

Cover design by Greg Smith of Black Lake Studio.

Published by Black Lake Press of Holland, Michigan. Black Lake Press is a division of Black Lake Studio, LLC. Direct inquiries to Black Lake Press at www.blacklakepress.com.

ISBN 978-0-9839602-8-7

Table of Contents

	About the Author	5
	Introduction	9
	Acknowledgements	11
All-time #1 Golf Myth:	"You Are Looking Up… Keep Your Head Down"	13
All-time #2 Golf Myth:	"Keep Your Eye On the Ball"	17
All-time #3 Golf Myth:	"Slow Down, You are Swinging Too Fast"	19
All-time #4 Golf Myth:	"Position the Ball Along Your Left Foot for Tee-Shots"	21
All-time #5 Golf Myth:	"In the Bunker– Aim Left and Open the Clubface"	23
All-time #5 Golf Myth:	(continued): "The Sand Shot Swing"	25
All-time #6 Golf Myth:	"The Club Needs to Go Under the Ball"	29

All-time #7 Golf Myth:	"Shift Your Weight (in the Backswing)"	31
	Conclusion	35
	FREE Golf Newsletter	37
	Special Bonus Offers	39

About the Author

Scott Seifferlein, PGA Golf Guru & Owner of GrandRapidsGolfLesson.com at The Highlands Golf Club, has been in the golf business for nineteen years. Scott has worked in Michigan, South Carolina, New York, and Florida. He has previously taught golf at White Lake Golf Club, Middle Bay Country Club, Advantage Golf Schools USA, Poxabogue Golf Center, and Mines Golf Course.

While holding the top instructor position at Middle Bay Country Club, Scott was featured in Donald Trump's book, *Trump: The Best Golf Advice I Ever Received.* He teaches each student differently based on their goals, physical limitations, and mindset. A major emphasis is placed on swinging the club with less effort.

A self taught golfer, Scott learned the hard way and has been where many of you are now. After eight years of trial and error, Scott began to receive golf instruction from some of the nation's best golf instructors. Combining eight years of learning the wrong way and sixteen years learning the right way and competing at a tier one level in both situations has given Scott an advantage over other golf instructors. He knows where you are coming from and can teach you to be successful from both sides. There is nothing you do in your golf swing that Scott has not already experienced in his own game, then corrected, and went on to win tournaments at a junior level, collegiate level, and professional level.

Professional Tournament Highlights

2000 West Michigan Chapter Champion

2000 West Michigan Chapter Assistants Champion

2001 West Michigan Chapter Assistants Champion

2003 Metropolitan PGA Assistant Tour Sands Point Event Champion

2004 U.S. Open Long Island Local Qualifier Medalist

Scott has conducted over four hundred clinics for both men and women, over two hundred junior clinics and camps, and over five thousand individual lessons. Scott was recently featured at the annual golf clinic for the Ferris State University President's Golf Outing.

Students have included Bill McCuddy of Fox News and John Bolaris of CBS News, New York. Scott's feature speaking engagement is titled "You're Not Looking Up & Other Golf Myths Revealed." This entertaining twenty to thirty minute clinic captures audiences with entertaining instruction, factual statistics, and audience participation.

"My sales were suffering in part because I avoided business golf outings before meeting Scott. Since taking golf lessons from Scott, my sales have doubled year over year. Scott helped me find the confidence on and off the course needed to excel in selling!"

—Dave B., Huntington Merchant Services

Introduction

For years, I faced the same struggles as you are now—always getting advice from my friends but never improving. "Play the ball off your front foot!" or "Slow Down," they would always tell me. But I just wasn't getting any better. Fortunately, I took a job in the golf business. At this point, I was able to work with some of America's top golf instructors, and I realized that they were not telling me any of the advice my friends told me. In fact often times they were telling me the exact opposite.

Before long, I was teaching golf as a member of the PGA of America. The clients I worked with would almost always tell me that they knew what their problems were. Time after time they would tell me some of the same things my friends had told me when I struggled with golf. So I started to use high speed video software and 3D wireless technology–www.K-Vest.com–to research what was really happening in my clients' golf swings. What I found will blow the lid off of all the common golf advice that is floating around the links.

As a result, I have made it my mission to Save Every Golfer on Planet Earth from Miserable Golf!! That is why I have created "Seven Golf Myths That Are Destroying Your Game." Take this very seriously, and never allow anyone to tell you any of the golf myths without first proving their advice.

Acknowledgements

Thank you to the following people who influenced & made this book possible...

Dennis Seifferlein, Ron English, Jeff Howland, Tom Underwood, Pat Eggling, Bobby Heins, Brad Bedortha, Bill Borgman, Kensey Snider, Charley Vandenberg, Frank Bensel, Colin Amaral, Doug Miller, Tim Shifflet, Buddy Whitten, Kim Shipman, Dan Kennedy, and everyone at GKIC, Joe Hallett, John Hughes, and all my present and past clients.

I know I have forgotten several important people. When you track me down, I will buy you a beer and offer my sincere apologies. My wife already says I owe her a beer.

"Scott, from the very first lesson, was able to greatly improve my golf swing. He is able to break a swing down into its various components that make sense and is easy to remember. He is great to work with."

—*Denice P., Korte Consulting, Grand Rapids*

Scott Seifferlein

The Game of Golf is filled with Myths

Through my nineteen years in the golf industry, I have compiled a list of the seven most common Golf Myths that cause you to slice the ball.

All-time #1 Golf Myth:
"You Are Looking Up... Keep Your Head Down"

Not so according to my article on page 111 in Donald Trump's self titled book, *Trump: The Best Golf Advice I Ever Received.* But if you go to any golf course and top the ball off the first tee, six other golfers will tell you to keep your head down. First of all, you didn't look up. Not before or at impact anyways. I have filmed thousands of golfers who say that they look up, and I have yet to meet one who actually looks up. I'll give you $100 if you find me a new client who does look up before or at impact. Contact me at 616.802.4969 or www.GrandRapidsGolfLesson.com to get your crisp Ben Franklin.

The reason your golf partners will tell you that you looked up is because of speed. No, your playing partners are not on drugs (well maybe), but I am talking about the speed of the golf swing. It simply happens too fast for the human eye to catch what is really happening through impact. Be cautious of anyone offering you golf advice if they are not using video that captures your swing with at least sixty frames per second. (Standard video captures at thrity frames per second.)

Your playing partners will first see that you hit a bad shot, and by the time they realize it is a bad shot, it will be a good half second after impact. At this point, you will be looking to see where your ball went. They will gain the perception that you were looking at impact. Not True.

Even if you were looking up at impact (which you were not), you would still hit good shots with the proper fundamentals in place. Search video of David Duval, Robert Allenby, Annika Sorenstam, and Charles Warren. All of these professional golfers look up faster than any Amateur I have ever met.

So why did you hit a lousy golf shot?

Some of the things that will cause you to top the ball include, a poor swing plane, poor posture, poor core stability, and a breakdown of the lead wrist. Call 616.802.4969 to find out which of these symptoms are giving you golf headaches.

Stop Slicing in Five Swings

Trying to keep your head down will prevent a good weight transfer and decrease your club head speed. So go out there, and never worry about keeping your head down again!

"I've been a slicer my whole life, and Scott showed me why and helped me to correct it."

—*Kurt M, Belmont*

All-time #2 Golf Myth:
"Keep Your Eye On the Ball"

Golfers have their eyes pointed anywhere from twelve to twenty-four inches behind the ball.

First of all, if your eye really was on the ball, it would be hard to hit it without serious retinal damage.

Second, if you had to keep your eye on the ball, blind people could not play golf (they do, check out www.BlindGolf.com).

Third, every good player out there has their eyes pointed anywhere from twelve to twenty-four inches behind the ball at the top of the golf swing. That is not to say that you should close your eyes or stare at the beverage cart girl while you are trying to smash 250-yard drives.

You just don't have to make extra effort to have your eyes pointed straight at the ball. Trying to keep your eyes pointed at the ball will lead to a reverse pivot and also may cause core stability issues, posture issues, and issues with getting the ball airborne.

All-time #3 Golf Myth:
"Slow down, You Are Swinging Too Fast"

This one really cracks me up. Go to any golf course or practice tee and listen for golfers who are "trying to slow down." Over 99% of amateur golfers have been told that they have to slow down.

Okay, here are the facts. The average golfer takes about 1.5 seconds from the start of the backswing to impact. Tour professionals typically take .9 seconds to 1.2 seconds. So why would we ever want to slow down when we are already a half a second slower than most Tour Pros?

This golf myth actually has some validity. However, it is often misinterpreted. When amateur golfers are told to slow down, it is actually the transition from the back-swing to the downswing in which they need to "slow down" to get better tempo. Unfortunately, they do not know what to slow down, and they either try to slow down their backswing, or they slow down the overall speed of their downswing which produces drives that would make Mr. Havercamp look like a long drive champion.

Many amateurs take a full second or more to complete their backswing. This is too slow and causes them to rush the transition into the downswing. In reality, they need to speed up their backswing. To achieve a swing tempo that is approximately one second from the start to impact, the backswing should take approximately .75 seconds. When the backswing is completed in this short time frame, there is enough time left to allow for a smooth transition into the downswing. The downswing should take approximately .25 seconds to reach impact. For those math majors out there, this is a three to one backswing to downswing ratio. This ratio is followed by most Tour Pros and will encourage a downswing that reaches maximum speed through impact. This swing will also appear smooth to your playing partners. Your speed will increase, and they will never tell you to slow down again!

Be sure to ask your PGA Instructor to film your golf swing and count your frames. Check to see how close you are to a three to one ratio and check the time it takes you to get from the start of the swing to impact. For more on this exciting topic go to: www.TourTempo.com

All-time #4 Golf Myth:
"Position the Ball Along Your Left Foot for Tee-Shots"

Do you feel like you are exerting a tremendous amount of effort to hit less than Herculean Drives? It could simply be your ball position. Many golfers I play with in Pro-ams lose a significant amount of distance by having the ball position too far forward. By the time they get to impact, they have passed the point of maximum club head speed.

Picture 1 *Picture 2*

As seen in Picture One, proper ball position for a Driver (if you are right handed) should be in an area between your left armpit and up to two inches to the right of your left armpit. This will also be about two to four inches inside your left heal. Playing the ball along your left foot is a big whammy. As I am showing in Picture Two, ball position along your left foot will cause you to open your shoulders and have poor spine angle. Open shoulders and a poor spine angle will give you a steep angle of approach to the ball. The results will be a topped shot, a pulled shot, and a pull slice.

"Scott, thanks for helping me have a great 2011 golf season! The three lessons I took from you early in the year really helped me take strokes off my handicap. The short game lessons were very beneficial. I trended between a zero and two handicap all year after starting the 2011 season as a six. Thanks again!"

—Shawn R

All-time #5 Golf Myth:
"In the Bunker–Aim Left and Open the Clubface"

Yeah Right! Only if you are a Tour Professional. This high risk bunker advice has shown up in golf magazines and golf schools for years. It is about time someone

Picture 1

Picture 2

publishes advice that will benefit the average golfer. So here it is...

As shown in Picture One and Picture Two above, aim your feet, hips and shoulders parallel to the target. Aim your clubface at your target. Your ball position will be slightly forward of center. This set-up will allow you to use the same swing you would use for your pitch shots. Your club will tend to bottom out in the center, allowing the sand to move your ball out of the bunker.

With this set-up, you may not be able to hit the high soft (tour like) bunker shot that makes you look like a hero. But you will be more consistent and avoid the hosel rocket shot that makes you want to bury your head in the sand.

"I have had a terrible problem golfing for the past three to four years which nobody has been able to fix. I had my first lesson last night from Scott Sefferlein, and with one little suggestion, he fixed me, and I'm hitting like I used to! If you need a coach, I highly recommend him, I have three more lessons. Then I'll be able to quit my day job and become a pro! (ha ha!)"

—*Wendi L., Grand Rapids*

All-time #5 Golf Myth: (continued): "The Sand Shot Swing"

With a set-up identical to your pitch shot, you will make your pitch shot swing. Keeping your legs relatively quiet and stable, swing the club back as you would a pitch shot. Notice the grip end of the club pointing at the ball in Picture One.

On the downswing, you do not want to follow common advice by swinging out to in. That would cause you to come over the top and hit the ball off the hosel. Make sure you swing on the same downswing path as you would a pitch shot as shown on the following page on Picture Two.

Picture 1   Picture 2

"I want to thank you for all you have done for Nick. The camp was excellent, and he enjoyed himself so much! Your knowledge, attention to detail, and patience in instruction are invaluable. We feel so blessed we were able to meet you at the range the first day we drove up. Our whirlwind introduction to this sport has been exciting. It has opened a whole new world for us...in more ways than you know. Nick went out and golfed 9 on his own on

Stop Slicing in Five Swings

Thursday…his first serious round of golf…and shot 50! I was very proud. He just loved it. He is continuing to work almost every day and loves it. Needless to say, we would recommend you highly to anyone."

—*Chris M.*

All-time #6 Golf Myth:
"The club Needs to Go Under the Ball"

Sure! If you want to hit a super high risk Phil Michelson Lob Shot. But seriously, Mr. 14 handicap, what in the world are you doing trying to hit a lob shot with your 5-iron? You have too many basic fundamentals to take care of first.

This golf myth has frustrated golfers for years. An attempt to get the club under the ball will add loft to your club head turning your 7-iron into a 9-iron at impact. To clear things up, the club does not actually go under the ball on a proper golf shot. The center of the clubface strikes the center of the ball while it is still on its way down (for irons). The ball then launches forward as the club reaches its low point in the swing arc approximately an inch or two ahead of where the ball was. As shown in the picture to the left, at no point is the club under the ball.

To find out if your irons are striking the ball correctly or going under it and adding loft, place a tee in the ground about two inches ahead of the ball. Leave the top of the tee exposed so that it is one quarter inch above the ground (not above the top of the grass). Play your shot and check to see if your club hit the tee. If it did not hit the tee your impact position was an ascending strike rather than a descending strike. Work towards a descending strike as this reduces your slice probability.

"Scott customizes his teaching methods to the unique needs of each and every client. My wife and I took semi-private lessons together from Scott. We are totally different golfers, but both of our games improved as a result of Scott's considerable expertise, along with his patient and caring style."

—Kurt Kimball, Grand Rapids

All-time #7 Golf Myth:
"Shift Your Weight (in the Backswing)"

For years, golfers have heard the advice to shift your weight and get behind the ball in the backswing. The result of this has helped create thousands of golfers who have too much weight into the outside of their back foot at the top of the backswing. This puts the golfer into a balance position in which it is very difficult to transfer weight back into the lead side of the body through impact. It would be similar to a football player trying to push off the line with the weight in their heels instead of the balls and toes of their feet.

If you have been told to shift your weight, check the two pictures above and make sure that you do not get into those positions.

Picture 1 *Picture 2*

"My buddy and I participated in a group session this past summer, and I used what you taught me the rest of season (light grip for my short irons). When the shots turned out, I could tell that I had the light grip and always said–that was a Scott Seifferlein shot."
—*Dave J., Grand Haven, MI*

As you can see in the picture below, the weight did not shift into the back foot, the back leg is leaning towards the target and

Stop Slicing in Five Swings

in a powerful position ready to fire towards the target. Watch your swing in a mirror and try your best to get into the position below. If you are having trouble, see a local fitness trainer to work on your flexibility.

"The best $400 dollars I ever spent."

—*Mike M.*

Conclusion

There you have it: "The Seven Golf Myths That Are Destroying Your Game." However, you are missing one final Golf Myth. The Grand-Daddy Golf Myth of them all. The one that will stop your slicing forever! E-mail: info@grandrapidsgolflesson.com to get this bonus Eight Golf Myth.

Free Golf Newsletter

Go to www.GrandRapidsGolfLesson.com and click on the newsletter link on the right side of the homepage.

Special Bonus Offers

I will pay you $200 to play golf. That's right...sign up for one of my one, two, or three day golf schools. Participate in the golf school, listen while you are there, stop slicing, and I will give you a graduation gift of $200 cold hard cash!

To learn more about these Seven Golf Myths and the necessary drills to correct your errors call 616.802.4969 to set up your learning experience.

Scott Seifferlein

Scott Seifferlein
PGA Golf Guru

The Highlands Golf Academy
2715 Leonard St. NW
Grand Rapids, MI 49504
www.GrandRapidsGolfLesson.com
www.HighlandsGR.com

616.802.4969

Made in the USA
Charleston, SC
21 October 2012